# Knit
# NEW YORK

## 10 ICONIC NEW YORK PROJECTS

Emma King

**COLLINS & BROWN**

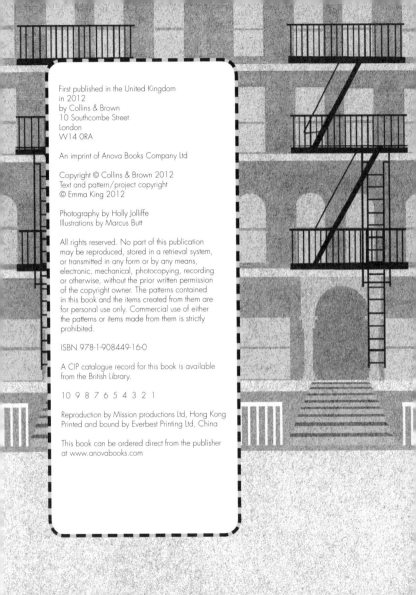

First published in the United Kingdom
in 2012
by Collins & Brown
10 Southcombe Street
London
W14 0RA

An imprint of Anova Books Company Ltd

Copyright © Collins & Brown 2012
Text and pattern/project copyright
© Emma King 2012

Photography by Holly Jolliffe
Illustrations by Marcus Butt

ISBN 978-1-908449-16-0

A CIP catalogue record for this book is available
from the British Library.

10 9 8 7 6 5 4 3 2 1

Reproduction by Mission productions Ltd, Hong Kong
Printed and bound by Everbest Printing Ltd, China

This book can be ordered direct from the publisher
at www.anovabooks.com

# CONTENTS

# NEW YORK, NEW YORK!

So good they named it twice, New York is one of the world's most iconic cities. Join us in a knitted celebration of its landmarks and symbols, but beware that deciding which project to knit first could be as difficult as deciding how to spend a day's sightseeing in New York!

You might like to start in the heart of Manhattan at the beautiful art deco Empire State Building, then take a walk along Broadway to the fabulously peculiar Flatiron Building. Don't let the skyscrapers take all your attention, though, or you may find yourself tripping over a fire hydrant or missing a walk/don't walk sign!

When you're ready for a break from the hustle and bustle of Manhattan, flag down a yellow taxi and head towards the ferry terminal. Take a trip on the Staten Island Ferry, staying on deck to enjoy a fabulous view of the Statue of Liberty. After a long day's sightseeing, treat yourself to a traditional New York delicacy, the humble hot dog, then knit yourself a souvenir of your trip to the Big Apple.

To keep you entertained while you're knitting, we have included some fun facts and a quick quiz about this magnificent city.

What are you waiting for?

Knit New York!

# THE BIG APPLE

## MEASUREMENTS
Height: 17cm (6¾in)
including stalk
Circumference: 67cm (26½in)

## YARN
Two 50g (115m/126yd) balls
of Rowan Cotton Glace in
Poppy 741 (A) and a small
amount in each of Shoot 814 (B)
and Toffee 843 (C)

## MATERIALS
One pair of 3mm (US 2/3)
knitting needles;
Two 3.25mm (US 3)
double-pointed needles;
Two stitch markers;
Tapestry needle;
Wadding (batting)

## TENSION (GAUGE)
26 sts and 34 rows to
10cm (4in) over stocking
(stockinette) stitch using
3mm (US 2/3) needles.

## ABBREVIATIONS
See pages 92–95 for
abbreviations and information
on the i-cord technique.

New York City's
nickname of the Big
Apple first became
popular in the 1920s
when *New York Morning
Telegraph* sports writer
John J. Fitz Gerald
began using the term.

**COLOUR KEY**
Yarn A = red
Yarn B = green
Yarn C = brown

**THE APPLE IS KNITTED IN TWO HALVES**

## HALF APPLE (make 2)
Using 3mm (US 2/3) needles and A, cast on 5 sts, leaving a long tail when casting on one of the halves (this will be used for sewing up the base of the apple when finishing).

**Row 1 (WS):** Purl.
**Row 2:** K1, [m1, k1] to end. (9 sts)
Repeat last two rows twice more. (33 sts)
**Row 7:** Purl.
**Row 8:** Knit.
**Row 9:** Purl.
**Row 10:** K1, [m1, k1] to end. (65 sts)
**Row 11:** Purl.
**Row 12:** Knit.
**Row 13:** Purl.
Repeat last two rows once more.
**Row 16:** K5, [m1, k5] to end. (77 sts)
**Row 17:** Purl.

**Row 18:** Knit.
**Row 19:** Purl.
Repeat last two rows three more times.
**Row 26:** K11, [m1, k11] to end. (83 sts)
Place a marker at each end of row 26.
**Row 27:** Purl.
**Row 28:** Knit.
**Row 29:** Purl.
Repeat last two rows until work measures 13cm (5¼in) from marked row.
**Next row:** K4, m1, k6, m1, [k9, m1] to last 10 sts, k6, m1, k4. (93 sts)
**Next row:** Purl.
**Next row:** Knit.
**Next row:** Purl.
Repeat last two rows once more.
**Next row:** K7, k2tog, [k9, k2tog] to last 7 sts, k to end. (85 sts)
**Next row:** Purl.
**Next row:** [K2, k2tog] to last st, k1. (64 sts)

**Next row:** Purl.
**Next row:** Knit.
**Next row:** Purl.
**Next row:** K1, k2tog, [k2, k2tog] to last st, k1. (48 sts)
Repeat last four rows once more. (36 sts)
**Next row:** Purl.
**Next row:** [K2tog] to end. (18 sts)
**Next row:** Purl.
Thread yarn through remaining stitches and pull together, leaving a long tail on one of the halves (this will be used for sewing up the top of the apple).

## LEAF

Using 3mm (US 2/3) needles and B, cast on 3 sts.
**Row 1 (WS):** K1, p1, k1.
**Row 2:** K1, m1, k1, m1, k1. (5 sts)
**Row 3:** K1, p3, k1.
**Row 4:** K2, m1, k1, m1, k2. (7 sts)
**Row 5:** K1, p5, k1.
**Row 6:** K3, m1, k1, m1, k3. (9 sts)
**Row 7:** K1, p7, k1.
**Row 8:** K4, m1, k1, m1, k4. (11 sts)
**Row 9:** K1, p9, k1.

Row 10: K5, m1, k1, m1, k5. (13 sts)
Row 11: K1, p11, k1.
Row 12: K6, m1, k1, m1, k6. (15 sts)
Row 13: K1, p13, k1.
Row 14: K7, m1, k1, m1, k7. (17 sts)
Row 15: K1, p15, k1.
Row 16: Knit.

Row 17: K1, p15, k1.
Row 18: K7, slip 2, k1, p2sso, k7. (15 sts)
Row 19: K1, p13, k1.
Row 20: K6, slip 2, k1, p2sso, k6. (13 sts)
Row 21: K1, p11, k1.
Row 22: K5, slip 2, k1, p2sso, k5. (11 sts)
Row 23: K1, p9, k1.
Row 24: K4, slip 2, k1, p2sso, k4. (9 sts)
Row 25: K1, p7, k1.
Row 26: K3, slip 2, k1, p2sso, k3. (7 sts)
Row 27: K1, p5, k1.
Row 28: K2, slip 2, k1, p2sso, k2. (5 sts)
Row 29: K1, p3, k1.
Row 30: K1, slip 2, k1, p2sso, k1. (3 sts)
Row 31: K1, p1, k1.
Row 32: Slip 2, k1, p2sso. (1 st)
Fasten off.

12

## STALK

The stalk is made from an i-cord. Using 3.25mm (US 3) double-pointed needles and C, cast on 5 sts, leaving a long tail for sewing the stalk to the apple. Knit every row using the i-cord technique until the cord measures 5cm (2in). Break off yarn, thread through stitches and pull together.

## FINISHING

Sew the two halves of the apple together using mattress stitch, starting at the cast-on edge (bottom) and finishing at the top, and leaving a small gap for stuffing. Insert wadding (batting), then finish the seam. There will be a circular gap at the top and bottom of the apple. Using the long tails of yarn that you left when making the two halves, sew around the edge of each gap, pulling tightly and encouraging the gaps to close. You might need to sew around each gap a few times. Sew the stalk and one pointed end of the leaf to the top centre of the apple.

# YELLOW TAXI

## MEASUREMENTS
Height: 13cm (5¼in)
Length: 30cm (12in)
Width: 15cm (6in)

## YARN
One 100g (274m/300yd) ball of
Patons Fab DK in each of Canary
2305 (A) and Black 2311 (B);
One 50g (85m/93yd) ball of
Rowan Handknit Cotton in
Bleached 263 (C) and a small
amount in Ice Water 239 (G);
Small amount of Rowan
Cotton Glace in each of Dawn
Grey 831 (D), Poppy 741 (E)
and Persimmon 832 (F)

## MATERIALS
One pair each of 4mm
(US 6) and 3.25mm
(US 3) knitting needles;
Stitch holder;
Four cardboard discs,
approx. 4cm (1½in) diameter;
Tapestry needle;
Sheets of wadding (batting)

## TENSION (GAUGE)
22 sts and 30 rows to 10cm
(4in) measured over stocking
(stockinette) stitch using
Patons Fab DK and 4mm
(US 6) needles.

## ABBREVIATIONS
See pages 92–95 for
abbreviations and information
on charts, the intarsia technique
and wrap stitches.

---

**COLOUR KEY**
Yarn A = yellow
Yarn B = black
Yarn C = white
Yarn D = light grey
Yarn E = red
Yarn F = orange
Yarn G = blue/grey

## DRIVER'S SIDE (left side)

Using 4mm (US 6) needles and A, cast on 65 sts.

**Row 1 (RS):** K20, p1, k10, p1, k1, p1, k10, p1, k20.

**Row 2:** P20, k1, p10, k1, p1, k1, p10, k1, p20.

Repeat last two rows nine more times.

Work rows 21 and 22 from the checked stripe chart provided, working row 21 as knit and row 22 as purl, and changing colours as indicated.

**Row 23:** Change back to A and knit to end.

**Row 24:** P20, k1, p10, k1, p1, k1, p10, k1, p20.

**Row 25:** K20, p1, k10, p1, k1, p1, k10, p1, k20.*

**Row 26:** Cast (bind) off 15 sts, patt 37 sts, turn, leaving remaining 13 sts on a holder. Working on these 37 sts only, work all ten rows of the driver's side chart provided, beginning with a knit row and working in stocking (stockinette) stitch (knit on RS, purl on WS) unless indicated otherwise. Change colours using the intarsia technique and shape as indicated. When completed, cast (bind) off.

Rejoin A to 13 sts on holder and cast (bind) them off.

## PASSENGER'S SIDE (right side)

Work as for driver's side until *.

**Row 26 (WS):** Cast (bind) off 13 sts, patt 37 sts, turn, leaving remaining 15 sts on a holder. Working on these 37 sts only, work all ten rows of the passenger's side chart provided, beginning with a knit row and working in stocking (stockinette) stitch (knit on RS, purl on WS) unless indicated otherwise. Change colours using the intarsia technique and shape as indicated. When completed, cast (bind) off.

Rejoin A to 15 sts on holder and cast (bind) them off.

**CHECKED STRIPE**

22

KEY   ■ Yarn B   □ Yarn C

## DRIVER'S SIDE

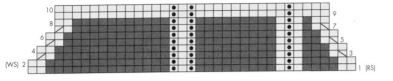

## PASSENGER'S SIDE

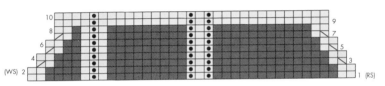

KEY

☐ Yarn A

■ Yarn B

● Purl on RS/knit on WS

⧄ ⧅ Dec 1

## REAR LIGHTS AND REAR BUMPER

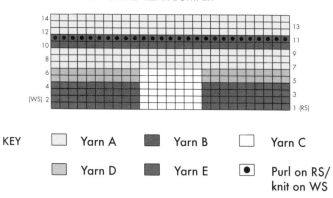

KEY

☐ Yarn A   ■ Yarn B   ☐ Yarn C

▨ Yarn D   ■ Yarn E   ⦿ Purl on RS/ knit on WS

## REAR WINDOW, ROOF AND WINDSCREEN

Using 4mm (US 6) needles, cast on 29 sts as follows: 2 sts in A, 25 sts in B, 2 sts in A. Keeping colours as set, work as follows:

**Row 1 (RS):** Knit.

**Row 2:** Purl.

Repeat last two rows five more times.

Using A only, continue as follows:

**Row 13:** Knit.

**Row 14:** Purl.

Repeat last two rows until work measures 20cm (8in) from cast-on edge, ending with a WS row. Rejoin B and repeat rows 1–12 once more.

Cast (bind) off.

## BOOT

Using 4mm (US 6) needles and A and with RS facing, pick up and knit 27 sts along cast-on edge of rear window.

**Row 1 (WS):** P3, k1, p19, k1, p3.

**Row 2:** K3, p1, k19, p1, k3.

Repeat last two rows seven more times and then row 1 once again.

Cast (bind) off.

## REAR LIGHTS AND REAR BUMPER

Using 4mm (US 6) needles and D and with RS facing, pick up and knit 27 sts along cast-off (bound-off) edge of boot.

**Row 1 (WS):** Knit.

Work all fourteen rows of the rear lights and rear bumper chart provided, beginning with a knit row and working in stocking (stockinette) stitch (knit on RS, purl on WS) unless indicated otherwise. Change colours using the intarsia technique as indicated. When completed, cast (bind) off.

The distinctive yellow taxi cab, both with and without a checked stripe, is an iconic symbol of New York City, with more than 13,000 official vehicles in operation.

## HEADLIGHTS AND FRONT BUMPER

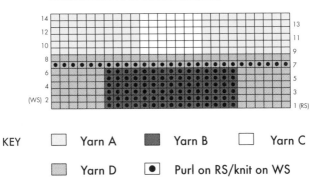

| KEY |  Yarn A | ■ Yarn B | □ Yarn C |
| | ▨ Yarn D | ● Purl on RS/knit on WS | |

20

## BONNET

Using 4mm (US 6) needles and A and with RS facing, pick up and knit 27 sts along cast-off (bound-off) edge of windscreen.
**Row 1 (WS):** P3, k1, p19, k1, p3.
**Row 2:** K3, p1, k19, p1, k3.
Repeat last two rows eight more times and then row 1 once again.
Cast (bind) off.

## HEADLIGHTS AND FRONT BUMPER

Using 4mm (US 6) needles and D and with RS facing, pick up and knit 27 sts along cast-off (bound-off) edge of bonnet.
**Row 1 (WS):** Knit.
Work all fourteen rows of the headlights and front bumper chart provided, beginning with a knit row and working in stocking (stockinette) stitch (knit on RS, purl on WS) unless indicated otherwise. Change colours using the intarsia technique as indicated. When completed, cast (bind) off.

## BASE

Using 4mm (US 6) needles and B and with RS facing, pick up and knit 27 sts along cast-off (bound-off) edge of rear bumper.

**Row 1 (WS):** Knit.
**Row 2:** Knit.
**Row 3:** Purl.

Repeat last two rows until work measures 16cm (6¼in) from cast-on edge.
Cast (bind) off.

Using 4mm (US 6) needles and B and with RS facing, pick up and knit 27 sts along cast-off (bound-off) edge of front bumper.

**Row 1 (WS):** Knit.
**Row 2:** Knit.
**Row 3:** Purl.

Repeat last two rows until work measures 16cm (6¼in) from cast-on edge.
Cast (bind) off.

## WHEELS (make 4)

Using 3.25mm (US 3) needles and B, cast on 9 sts.

**Row 1 (RS):** Knit.
**Next row:** *P6, wrap st, turn, k to end.

Repeat from * until work measures 3cm (1¼in) from cast-on edge, then cast (bind) off. The knitted piece will naturally curl into a tyre shape. Encourage

it to do so, sewing along the cast-on edge. You will now have a circular piece of knitting that curls in at the edges. Insert a cardboard disc into the knitted circle, using the curling edges to trap the disc inside. Then run a piece of yarn B all the way around the edge of the circle (a running stitch) and pull the two ends together – this will act like a drawstring and pull the knitted circle together, covering the disc. Fasten securely, leaving an end to sew the wheel to the taxi.

## 'TAXI' SIGN

Using 3.25mm (US 3) needles, cast on 17 sts as follows: 4 sts in F, 7 sts in C, 4 sts in F. Keeping colours as set, work as follows:

**Row 1 (RS):** Knit.
**Row 2:** Purl.

Repeat last two rows twice more.

**Row 7:** Purl (this creates a ridge).
**Row 8:** Purl.
**Row 9:** Knit.
**Row 10:** Purl.

Repeat last two rows once more and then row 9 once again.
Cast (bind) off.

## FINISHING

Using yarn B, embroider 'TAXI' onto the centre front and back of the taxi sign. Using yarn G, embroider 'NYC' onto the front and rear registration plates. Make sure that all of the lettering will be the correct way up when the pieces are assembled.

You will have three main pieces for the taxi: two side panels and one long section that incorporates the first half of the base, front lights/bumper, bonnet, windscreen, roof, rear window, boot, rear lights/bumper and the other half of the base. Using mattress stitch for all the seams, join both side panels to the long section, starting at the rear bumper and ending at the front bumper. Then sew the base into position, leaving the cast-on/cast-off (bound-off) edges of the base open. Use this opening to insert sheets of wadding (batting), then sew the seam of the base. Using sheets of wadding rather than loose toy stuffing will enable you to achieve a 'squarer' finish.

Sew all four wheels onto the taxi. Fold the taxi sign in half along the ridge and sew the sign into place towards the front of the roof.

**KNIT NEW YORK?**
**QUIZ NEW YORK**
**Can you answer these questions about New York? If you get stuck, the answers are on page 96.**

1. New York City is made up of five boroughs. What are their names and which are the largest and smallest in terms of land area?

2. Which four streets form the boundaries of Times Square?

3. Name NYC's two major baseball and two major American football teams.

4. New York's subway system is one of the most extensive in the world. Guess how many stations there are.

# STATUE OF LIBERTY

## MEASUREMENTS

Height: 46cm (18in) from base
of pedestal to top of torch
Pedestal: 12cm (4¾in) square

## YARN

Three 50g (140m/153yd)
balls of Rowan Siena 4 Ply in
Celadan 669 (A), two balls
in Oak 659 (B) and a small
amount in Greengage 661 (C)

## MATERIALS

One pair each of 3mm
(US 2/3) and 4mm (US 6)
knitting needles;
Two 2.5mm (US 1/2)
double-pointed needles;
Tapestry needle;
Wadding (batting) and foam;
Hair grip (bobby pin);
Small piece of cardboard to
place inside tablet (optional)

## TENSION (GAUGE)

28 sts and 38 rows to 10cm
(4in) measured over stocking
(stockinette) stitch using 3mm
(US 2/3) needles.

## ABBREVIATIONS

See pages 92–95 for
abbreviations and information
on the i-cord technique.

## NOTE

The dress and sash form the
body of the statue; the only body
parts that are knitted are the
arms and head. The left arm
is made in two pieces and the
right arm in one piece.

**COLOUR KEY**
Yarn A = blue green
Yarn B = beige
Yarn C = green

## DRESS (make 2)

Using 3mm (US 2/3) needles
and A, cast on 40 sts.
**Row 1 (WS):** Purl.
**Row 2:** K2, [m1, k2] to end.
(59 sts)
**Row 3:** Purl.
**Row 4:** Knit.
**Row 5:** Purl.
**Row 6:** K2, m1, [k5, m1] to
last 2 sts, k2. (71 sts)
**Row 7:** Purl.
**Row 8:** Knit.
**Row 9:** Purl.
Repeat last two rows six
more times.
**Row 22:** K2, k2tog, [k11, k2tog]
to last 2 sts, k2. (65 sts)
**Row 23:** Purl.
**Row 24:** Knit.
**Row 25:** Purl.
Repeat last two rows four
more times.
**Row 34:** K4, k2tog, [k9, k2tog]
to last 4 sts, k4. (59 sts)
**Row 35:** Purl.
**Row 36:** Knit.
**Row 37:** Purl.
Repeat last two rows twice
more.
**Row 42:** K1, k2tog, [k3, k2tog]
to last st, k1. (47 sts)
**Row 43:** Purl.
**Row 44:** Knit.
**Row 45:** Purl.

Repeat last two rows three
more times.
**Row 52:** K6, k2tog, [k9, k2tog]
to last 6 sts, k6. (43 sts)
**Row 53:** Purl.
**Row 54:** Knit.
**Row 55:** Purl.
Repeat last two rows five
more times.
**Row 66:** K3, k2tog, [k5, k2tog]
to last 3 sts, k3. (37 sts)
**Row 67:** Purl.
**Row 68:** Knit.
**Row 69:** Purl.
Repeat last two rows twice more.
**Row 74:** K2tog, [k3, k2tog] to
end. (29 sts)
**Row 75:** Purl.
**Row 76:** Knit.
**Row 77:** Purl.
Cast (bind) off, knitting two
stitches together at each end.

## LEFT SLEEVE

Using 3mm (US 2/3) needles
and A, cast on 25 sts.
**Row 1 (RS):** Knit.
**Row 2:** Purl.
Repeat last two rows once more.
**Row 5:** K5, [m1, k5] to end.
(29 sts)
**Row 6:** Purl.
**Row 7:** Knit.
**Row 8:** Purl.
Repeat last two rows once more.

**Row 11:** K1, m1, [k3, m1] to last st, k1. (39 sts)
**Row 12:** Purl.
**Row 13:** Knit.
**Row 14:** Purl.
Repeat last two rows twice more.
**Row 19:** K3, [m1, k3] to end. (51 sts)
**Row 20:** Purl.
**Row 21:** Knit.
**Row 22:** Purl.
Repeat last two rows four more times.
**Row 31:** Create a tuck in the fabric by knitting each of the 51 sts of this row together with the back loop of each corresponding stitch on the fourth previous row. When counting four rows back, include the row on the needle.

**Row 32:** Purl.
**Row 33:** Knit.
**Row 34:** Purl.
Repeat last two rows twice more.
**Row 39:** Create tuck as before.
**Row 40:** Purl.
**Row 41:** K2, k2tog, [k3, k2tog] to last 2 sts, k2. (41 sts)
**Row 42:** Purl.
Cast (bind) off.

### MAKING THE TUCKS

The tucks in the sleeves are made by knitting the stitches of the current row to the back loops of the corresponding stitches on a previous row. You may find it helpful to use a third needle to pick up the stitches of the previous row. This makes the knitting much easier and ensures that you have found all of the stitches before you start.

## RIGHT SLEEVE

Using 3mm (US 2/3) needles and A, cast on 25 sts.
**Row 1 (RS):** Knit.
**Row 2:** Purl.
Repeat last two rows once more.
**Row 5:** K5, [m1, k5] to end. (29 sts)
**Row 6:** Purl.
**Row 7:** K1, m1, [k3, m1] to last st, k1. (39 sts)
**Row 8:** Purl.
**Row 9:** Knit.
**Row 10:** Purl.
**Row 11:** K3, [m1, k3] to end. (51 sts)
**Row 12:** Purl.
**Row 13:** Knit.
**Row 14:** Purl.
Repeat last two rows once more.
**Row 17:** Create tuck as before.
**Row 18:** Purl.
**Row 19:** Knit.
**Row 20:** Purl.
Repeat last two rows once more.
Repeat rows 17–22 once more.
**Row 29:** K2, k2tog, [k3, k2tog] to last 2 sts, k2. (41 sts)
**Row 30:** Purl.
Cast (bind) off.

## SASH (make 2)

Using 3mm (US 2/3) needles and A, cast on 9 sts.
**Row 1 (WS):** Purl.
**Row 2:** K1, [m1, k1] to end. (17 sts)
**Row 3:** Purl.
**Row 4:** Knit.
**Row 5:** Purl.
Repeat last two rows three more times.
**Row 12:** K1, m1, [k3, m1] to last st, k1. (23 sts)
**Row 13:** Purl.
**Row 14:** Knit.
**Row 15:** Purl.
Repeat last two rows three more times.
**Row 22:** K1, m1, [k4, m1] twice, k5, m1, [k4, m1] twice, k1. (29 sts)
**Row 23:** Purl.
**Row 24:** Knit.
**Row 25:** Purl.
Repeat last two rows three more times.
**Row 32:** K2, m1, [k5, m1] to last 2 sts, k2. (35 sts)
**Row 33:** Purl.
**Row 34:** Knit.
**Row 35:** Purl.
Repeat last two rows three more times.
**Row 42:** K5, [m1, k5] to end. (41 sts)

The statue represents Libertas, the Roman goddess of freedom. Designed by French sculptor Frédéric Bartholdi, it was a gift from France to the United States to commemorate the Declaration of Independence.

Row 43: Purl.
Row 44: Knit.
Row 45: Purl.
Repeat last two rows four
more times.
Row 54: K3, m1, [k5, m1] to
last 3 sts, k3. (49 sts)
Row 55: Purl.
Row 56: Knit.
Row 57: Purl.
Repeat last two rows four
more times.
Row 66: K1, k2tog, [k7, k2tog]
to last st, k1. (43 sts)
Row 67: Purl.
Row 68: Knit.
Row 69: Purl.

Repeat last two rows twice more.
Row 74: K3, [k2tog, k3] to end.
(35 sts)
Row 75: Purl.
Row 76: Knit.
Row 77: Purl.
Repeat last two rows once more.
Row 80: K4, k2tog, [k3, k2tog]
to last 4 sts, k4. (29 sts)
Row 81: Purl.
Row 82: Knit.
Row 83: Purl.
Row 84: K1, [k3tog] to last st,
k1. (11 sts)
Row 85: Purl.
Cast (bind) off.

## LEFT ARM – FIRST PIECE
Using 3mm (US 2/3) needles
and A, cast on 5 sts.
Row 1 (WS): Purl
Row 2: K1, [m1, k1] to end.
(9 sts)
Row 3: Purl.
Row 4: Knit.
Row 5: Purl.
Repeat last two rows eight
more times.
Row 22: Cast 14 sts onto left
needle and knit across all stitches
to end. (23 sts)
Row 23: Purl.
Row 24: Knit.
Row 25: Purl.
Repeat last two rows twice more.
Cast (bind) off.

## LEFT ARM – SECOND PIECE
Using 3mm (US 2/3) needles
and A, cast on 23 sts.
Row 1 (RS): Knit.
Row 2: Purl.
Repeat last two rows twice more.
Row 7: Cast (bind) off 14 sts,
k to end. (9 sts)
Row 8: Purl.
Row 9: Knit.
Row 10: Purl.
Repeat last two rows seven
more times.

**Row 25:** K1, [k2tog] to end.
(5 sts)
**Row 26:** Purl.
Cast (bind) off.

### RIGHT ARM
Using 3mm (US 2/3) needles
and A, cast on 8 sts.
**Row 1 (WS):** Purl.
**Row 2:** K1, [m1, k1] to end.
(15 sts)
**Row 3:** Purl.
**Row 4:** Knit.
**Row 5:** Purl.
Repeat last two rows fifteen
more times.
**Row 36:** K1, [k2tog] to end.
(8 sts)
**Row 37:** Purl.
Do not cast (bind) off. Thread
yarn through remaining sts and
pull together.

### THE KNITTY GRITTY
### Here are some top facts
### about the Statue of Liberty.

Completed in 1886, the
statue stands at just over
93m (305ft) high from base
of pedestal foundations to
tip of torch flame.

Each spike on the crown
represents one of the seven
continents of the world.

The inner steel structure
was designed by French
engineer Gustave Eiffel,
who went on to build the
Eiffel Tower in Paris.

The patinated green copper
that covers the exterior of
the statue is less than the
thickness of two pennies.
The torch flame is covered
with 24k gold.

## HEAD
Using 3mm (US 2/3) needles and A, cast on 5 sts.
**Row 1 (WS):** Purl.
**Row 2:** K1, [m1, k1] to end. (9 sts)
**Row 3:** Purl.
**Row 4:** K1, [m1, k1] to end. (17 sts)
**Row 5:** Purl.
**Row 6:** Knit.
**Row 7:** Purl.
**Row 8:** K1, [m1, k1] to end. (33 sts)
**Row 9:** Purl.
**Row 10:** Knit.
**Row 11:** Purl.
**Row 12:** K16, slip 1, k16.
Repeat last two rows five more times.
**Row 23:** Purl.
**Row 24:** [K2tog] eight times, slip 1, [k2tog] to end. (17 sts)
**Row 25:** Purl.
**Row 26:** [K2tog] four times, slip 1, [k2tog] to end. (9 sts)
**Row 27:** Purl.
Do not cast (bind) off. Thread yarn through remaining sts and pull together.

## CROWN
Using 3mm (US 2/3) needles and A, cast on 13 sts.
**Row 1 (WS):** Purl.

**Row 2:** K1, [m1, k1] to end. (25 sts)
**Row 3:** K1, [p1, k1] to end.
**Row 4:** Inc 1 purlwise, [k1, p1] to last 2 sts, k1, inc 1 purlwise. (27 sts)
**Row 5:** P1, [k1, p1] to end.
**Row 6:** Inc 1 knitwise, [p1, k1] to last 2 sts, p1, inc 1 knitwise. (29 sts)
**Row 7:** K1, [p1, k1] to end.
Cast (bind) off in pattern.

## CROWN SPIKES
### (make 7)
Each spike is made from an i-cord. Using 2.5mm (US 1/2) double-pointed needles and A, cast on 3 sts. Knit every row using the i-cord technique until the cord measures 4cm (1½in). K3tog and fasten off, leaving a long tail to sew the spike to the crown.

## TORCH HANDLE
The torch handle is made from an i-cord. Using 2.5mm (US 1/2) double-pointed needles and A, cast on 5 sts. Knit every row using the i-cord technique until the cord measures 5cm (2in). Cast (bind) off.

## TORCH BOWL

The torch bowl is made from an i-cord. Using 2.5mm (US 1/2) double-pointed needles and A, cast on 5 sts. Knit every row using the i-cord technique until the cord measures 7cm (2¾in). Cast (bind) off.

## TORCH FLAME

Using 2.5mm (US 1/2) double-pointed needles and C, cast on 4 sts.

**Row 1 (RS):** Purl.
**Row 2:** K1, [m1, k1] to end.
(7 sts)
Continue using the i-cord technique from here onwards:
**Row 3:** Knit.
**Row 4:** Knit.
**Row 5:** Knit.
**Row 6:** Knit.
**Row 7:** K2tog, k3, k2tog. (5 sts)
**Row 8:** Knit.
**Row 9:** Knit.
**Row 10:** K2tog, k1, k2tog.
(3 sts)
**Row 11:** Knit.
**Row 12:** K3tog.
Fasten off.

## TABLET

Using 3mm (US 2/3) needles and A, cast on 23 sts.
**Row 1 (RS):** K11, slip 1, k11.
**Row 2:** Purl.
Repeat last two rows until work measures 6cm (2½in) from cast-on edge.
Cast (bind) off.

## PEDESTAL SIDES

Using 4mm (US 6) needles and B held double, cast on 90 sts.
**Row 1 (RS):** P9, k2, slip 1, k2, [p17, k2, slip 1, k2] three times, p10.
**Row 2:** K10, p5, [k17, p5] three times, k9.
Repeat last two rows until work measures 14cm (5½in) from cast-on edge.
Cast (bind) off in pattern.

## PEDESTAL TOP

Using 4mm (US 6) needles and B held double, cast on 23 sts.
**Row 1 (RS):** Knit.
**Row 2:** Purl.
Repeat last two rows until work measures 11cm (4¼in) from cast-on edge.
Cast (bind) off.

## PEDESTAL BASE

Work as for pedestal top.

## FINISHING
### Dress, Sleeves and Sash

Sew the two pieces of the dress together along the cast-off (bound-off) edges; this forms the shoulder/neck area. Then sew the side seams, leaving a 4cm (1½in) gap at the top of each side seam just below the shoulder for the armholes. Sew the side seams of both sleeves and then join each sleeve to the armhole of the dress, noting which is left and which is right. Join the two pieces of the sash by sewing the cast-on edges together and the cast-off (bound-off) edges together. Drape the sash over the left shoulder of the dress, slip stitching it to the left shoulder seam to help keep it in place.

**USE YARN B DOUBLE FOR MAKING THE PEDESTAL**

## Arms

With right sides facing, sew the two pieces of the left arm together, leaving a small gap for stuffing. Insert wadding (batting) and then finish the seam. Insert the left arm into the left sleeve; it should be a snug fit in the armhole. Use a few stitches to help keep the top of the arm in the armhole. Do the same for the right arm/sleeve.

## Head and Crown

Sew the seam of the head, leaving a small gap for stuffing. Insert wadding (batting), then finish the seam. The line of slipped stitches denotes the nose. Stitch the seven spikes to the wrong side of the crown, aligning them with the cast-on edge so that 2cm (¾in) of each spike is sewn to the crown and the remaining 2cm (¾in) overhangs. Position one spike at each end of the crown and space the remaining five spikes evenly in between. Attach the crown to the front of the head, centring it to the slip stitch nose.

## Torch

Assemble the bowl by slip stitching the cast-on and cast-off (bound-off) edges of the i-cord together to form a ring. Slip stitch the cast-off (bound-off) edge of the handle to the centre of the ring (bowl). Sew the cast-on edge of the flame into the centre of the bowl. Stitch the handle of the torch to the 'hand' of the right arm. Insert a hair grip (bobby pin) into the handle of the torch until it disappears and sticks into the arm; this will make the torch stand upright.

### Tablet

Fold the tablet in half along the slip stitch ridge and sew the three seams together, inserting a piece of foam or cardboard to help keep the shape. Place the tablet under the left arm and slip stitch both tablet and arm into place.

### Pedestal and Final Assembly

The sides of the pedestal are knitted in one piece, with slipped stitches creating the four corners. Join the two side edges of the knitted piece to complete the structure. Join the top onto the pedestal by sewing it to the cast-off (bound-off) edge of the pedestal sides. Insert foam and then sew the base to the cast-on edges of the pedestal sides.

Place a block of foam under the dress of the statue to create the body. The top edges of the foam will help to shape the shoulders and will enable the statue to stand up. The dress should drape over the foam. Making sure that the drape is not lost, attach the statue to the pedestal by sewing the cast-on edges of the dress to the top of the pedestal, making sure that some of the pedestal top is still visible all the way around. Sew the head to the centre of the shoulder seam.

# EMPIRE STATE BUILDING

## MEASUREMENTS

Height: 56cm (22in)
Width: 27cm (10½in)
Depth: 14cm (5½in)

## YARN

Three 50g (120m/131yd) balls
of Rowan Belle Organic DK by
Amy Butler in Zinc 017 (A) and
two balls in Slate 015 (B)

## MATERIALS

One pair of 4mm (US 6)
knitting needles;
Two 4mm (US 6)
double-pointed needles;
Tapestry needle;
Sheets of wadding (batting)

## TENSION (GAUGE)

22 sts and 30 rows to 10cm
(4in) measured over stocking
(stockinette) stitch using
4mm (US 6) needles.

## ABBREVIATIONS

See pages 92-95 for
abbreviations and information
on charts, the intarsia technique
and the i-cord technique.

### COLOUR KEY
Yarn A = light grey
Yarn B = dark grey

## TOWER SECTION 1

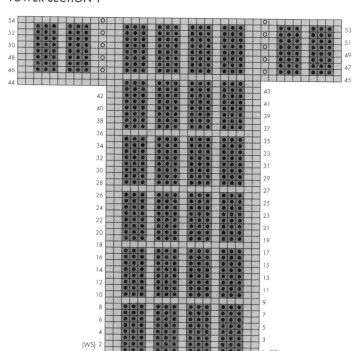

KEY

☐ Yarn A

▨ Yarn B

⦿ Purl on RS/knit on WS

▢ Slip 1 purlwise

40

## TOWER SECTION 2

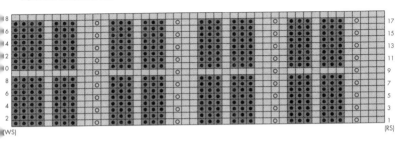

(WS)  2 4 6 8 10 12 14 16 18

17 15 13 11 9 7 5 3 1 (RS)

## TOWER SECTION 3

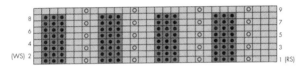

(WS) 2 4 6 8

9 7 5 3 1 (RS)

## TOWER SECTION 1 (make 2)

Using 4mm (US 6) needles
and A, cast on 19 sts.
Work rows 1–54 from the
tower section 1 chart provided,
beginning with a knit row and
working in stocking (stockinette)
stitch (knit on RS, purl on WS)
unless indicated otherwise.
Change colours using the intarsia
technique as indicated. You will
need to cast on 11 sts at the
beginning of row 44 and cast
on 10 sts at the beginning of
row 45. When completed,
repeat rows 46–54 of the chart
five more times. Cast (bind) off.

## TOWER SECTION 2

Using 4mm (US 6) needles
and A, cast on 46 sts.
Work rows 1–18 from the
tower section 2 chart provided,
beginning with a knit row and
working in stocking (stockinette)
stitch (knit on RS, purl on WS)
unless indicated otherwise.
Change colours using the
intarsia technique as indicated.
When completed, continue using
A only as follows:
**Row 19:** K1, k2tog, slip 1,
k2tog, k5, k2tog, slip 1, k2tog,
k7, k2tog, slip 1, k2tog, k5,
k2tog, slip 1, k2tog, k8. (38 sts)

**Row 20:** P2tog, p1, p2tog, k3, p2tog, p1, p2tog, k5, p2tog, p1, p2tog, k3, p2tog, p1, p2tog, k7. (30 sts)
**Row 21:** K2tog, [k2, k2tog] to end. (22 sts)
**Row 22:** P2tog, [p2, p2tog] to end. (16 sts)
Cast (bind) off.

## TOWER SECTION 3

Using 4mm (US 6) needles and A, cast on 30 sts.
Work rows 1–9 from the tower section 3 chart provided, beginning with a knit row and working in stocking (stockinette) stitch (knit on RS, purl on WS) unless indicated otherwise.
Change colours using the intarsia technique as indicated. When completed, continue using A only as follows:
**Row 10:** K2tog, [k2, k2tog] to end. (22 sts)
**Row 11:** P2tog, [p2, p2tog] to end. (16 sts)
**Row 12:** [K2tog] to end. (8 sts)
Do not cast (bind) off. Thread yarn through remaining stitches and pull together.

SEE PAGES 40–41 FOR TOWER SECTION CHARTS

## BASE SECTION 1
### (make 2)

Using 4mm (US 6) needles and A, cast on 61 sts.
Work rows 1–18 from the base section 1 chart provided, beginning with a knit row and working in stocking (stockinette) stitch (knit on RS, purl on WS) unless indicated otherwise.
Change colours using the intarsia technique as indicated. When completed, continue using A only as follows:
**\*Row 19:** K2tog, k7, k2tog, slip 1, k2tog, k33, k2tog, slip 1, k2tog, k7, k2tog. (55 sts)
**Row 20:** P2tog, p5, p2tog, p1, p2tog, p31, p2tog, p1, p2tog, p5, p2tog. (49 sts)
**Row 21:** K2tog, k3, k2tog, slip 1, k2tog, k29, k2tog, slip 1, k2tog, k3, k2tog. (43 sts)

**Row 22:** P2tog, p1, p2tog, p1, p2tog, p27, p2tog, p1, p2tog, p1, p2tog. (37 sts)
**Row 23:** K2tog, k2tog, slip 1, k2tog, k25, k2tog, slip 1, k2tog, k2tog. (31 sts)
**Row 24:** P2tog, p1, p2tog, p1, p2tog, p23, p2tog, p1, p2tog, p1, p2tog. (25 sts)
Cast (bind) off**.

## BASE SECTION 2
## (make 2)

Using 4mm (US 6) needles and A, cast on 61 sts.
Work rows 1–36 from the base section 2 chart provided, beginning with a knit row and working in stocking (stockinette) stitch (knit on RS, purl on WS) unless indicated otherwise.
Change colours using the intarsia technique as indicated.
When completed, continue using A only, working as for base section 1 from * to **.

SEE PAGES
44–45 FOR
BASE SECTION
CHARTS

## BASE SECTION 3
## (make 2)

Using 4mm (US 6) needles and A, cast on 41 sts.
Work rows 1–45 from the base section 3 chart provided, beginning with a knit row and working in stocking (stockinette) stitch (knit on RS, purl on WS) unless indicated otherwise.
Change colours using the intarsia technique as indicated.
When completed, continue using A only as follows:
**Row 46:** Purl.
**Row 47:** K5, k2tog, slip 1, k2tog, k21, k2tog, slip 1, k2tog, k5. (37 sts)
**Row 48:** P2tog, p2, p2tog, p1, p2tog, p19, p2tog, p1, p2tog, p2, p2tog. (31 sts)
**Row 49:** K2, k2tog, slip 1, k2tog, k17, k2tog, slip 1, k2tog, k2. (27 sts)
**Row 50:** P1, p2tog, p1, p2tog, p15, p2tog, p1, p2tog, p1. (23 sts)
**Row 51:** K2tog, slip 1, k2tog, k13, k2tog, slip 1, k2tog. (19 sts)
**Row 52:** [K2tog] twice, k to last 4 sts, [k2tog] twice. (15 sts)
Cast (bind) off.

BASE SECTION 1

BASE SECTION 2

44

## BASE SECTION 3

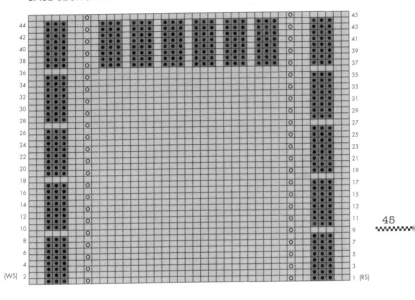

KEY

Yarn A

Yarn B

● Purl on RS/knit on WS

○ Slip 1 purlwise

Indicates seam lines
where pieces of the base
are sewn together during
finishing (see page 47)

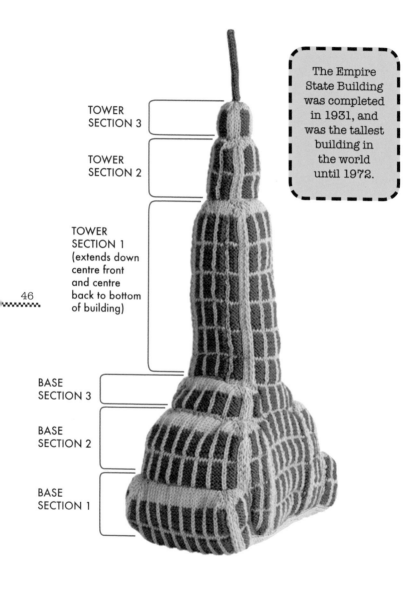

TOWER
SECTION 3

TOWER
SECTION 2

TOWER
SECTION 1
(extends down
centre front
and centre
back to bottom
of building)

46

BASE
SECTION 3

BASE
SECTION 2

BASE
SECTION 1

The Empire
State Building
was completed
in 1931, and
was the tallest
building in
the world
until 1972.

## ANTENNA

The antenna is made from an i-cord. Using 4mm (US 6) double-pointed needles and B, cast on 5 sts. Knit every row using the i-cord technique until the cord measures 8cm (3¼in). Break off yarn, thread through stitches and pull together.

## KNITTED BASE
### (to go underneath building)

Using 4mm (US 6) needles and A, cast on 25 sts.

**Row 1 (RS):** Knit.

**Row 2:** Purl.

Repeat last two rows until work measures 27cm (10½in) from cast-on edge. Cast (bind) off.

## FINISHING

Identify each piece of the building – base section 1, base section 2 and so on. The plain light grey (yarn A) stocking (stockinette) stitch areas of base sections 2 and 3 (indicated by red outline on charts on pages 44–45) will not be visible once the building is assembled – other sections of the base will be sewn around the indicated seam lines to cover these plain areas.

Sew the cast-off (bound-off) and both side edges of base section 1 to the indicated plain area of base section 2. Sew the cast-off (bound-off) and both side edges of base section 2 to the indicated plain area of base section 3. Repeat for the other side of the base.

Sew the side edges of rows 1– 43 of tower section 1 to the side edges of base section 3. Do this for the front and back of the tower. Sew the cast-on edges of rows 44 and 45 of tower section 1 to the cast-off (bound-off) edge of base section 3. Do this for the front and back of the tower. Sew the side seams of tower section 1 together, then do the same for tower section 2 and then tower section 3. Sew the antenna to the top of tower section 3, closing the top of the tower as you do so.

Insert wadding (batting) into the tower, then sew tower sections 2 and 3 on top of section 1; make sure that the stuffing reaches to the top. Cut sheets of wadding (batting) to insert into the base, using the stuffing to create shape. Finally, attach the knitted base under the building. The base is slightly shorter than the width of the tower base to encourage the sides to 'draw in' slightly.

# STATEN ISLAND FERRY

## MEASUREMENTS

Height: 28cm (11in)
Length: 56cm (22in)
Width: 20cm (8in)

## MATERIALS

Four 50g (85m/93yd) balls
of Rowan Handknit Cotton in
each of Florence 350 (A),
Black 252 (B), Slate 347 (C)
and Bleached 263 (D);
Small amount of Rowan
Siena 4 Ply in each of
White 651 (E), Chilli 666 (F)
and Mariner 672 (G)

## MATERIALS

One pair each of 4mm
(US 6) and 3mm (US 2/3)
knitting needles;
Two 2.5mm (US 1/2)
double-pointed needles;
Four stitch markers;
Tapestry needle;
Foam and wadding (batting);
Thin dowelling (or similar),
approx. 13cm (5¼in) long

## TENSION (GAUGE)

20 sts and 28 rows to 10cm
(4in) measured over stocking
(stockinette) stitch using
Rowan Handknit Cotton and
4mm (US 6) needles.

## ABBREVIATIONS

See pages 92-95 for
abbreviations and information
on charts, the intarsia
technique, wrap stitches
and the i-cord technique.

## NOTE

Slip all slipped stitches purlwise.

---

**COLOUR KEY**

Yarn A = orange
Yarn B = black
Yarn C = grey
Yarn D = white
Yarn E = white
Yarn F = red
Yarn G = blue

SEE PAGES 52–53 FOR LEFT AND RIGHT SIDE CHART

## LEFT SIDE

Using 4mm (US 6) needles and B, cast on 87 sts.

**Row 1 (RS):** Knit.

**Row 2:** Purl.

**Row 3:** Inc 1, k to last st, inc 1. (89 sts)

**Row 4:** Purl.

**Row 5:** Inc 1, k to last st, inc 1. (91 sts)

**Row 6:** Inc 1, p to last st, inc 1. (93 sts)

Repeat last two rows once more, then row 6 once again. (99 sts)

**Row 10:** Purl.*

Work rows 11–50 from the side chart provided, beginning with a knit row and working in stocking (stockinette) stitch (knit on RS, purl on WS). For the left side of the ferry, work all knit rows (RS rows) from right to left and all purl rows (WS rows) from left to right. Change colours using the intarsia technique and shape as indicated. When rows 11–50 of the chart have been completed, continue in A only as follows:

**Next row (RS):** Cast (bind) off 2 sts, k12, turn and work on these 12 sts only as follows:

**Next row:** Purl.

**Next row:** K2tog, k to last 2 sts k2tog. (10 sts)

**Next row:** Purl.

Cast (bind) off.

With RS facing, rejoin A to remaining 73 sts and work as follows:

**Next row:** Cast (bind) off 55 sts, k to end. Place a marker at each end of these 55 sts.

**Next row:** Cast (bind) off 2 sts, p16, turn and work on these 16 sts only as follows:

**Next row:** Purl.

**Next row:** K2tog, k to last 2 sts, k2tog. (14 sts)

**Next row:** Purl.

Cast (bind) off.

## RIGHT SIDE

Using 4mm (US 6) needles and B, cast on 87 sts.

Work as for left side until *. Work rows 11–50 from the side chart as before, but this time work all knit rows (RS rows) from left to right and all purl rows (WS rows) from right to left. This is a clever way of creating two sides for the ferry that are the mirror image of each other. When rows 11–50 of the chart have been completed, continue in A only as follows:

**Next row (RS):** Cast (bind) off 2 sts, k16, turn and work on these 16 sts only as follows:

**Next row:** Purl.

**Next row:** K2tog, k to last 2 sts, k2tog. (14 sts)
**Next row:** Purl.
Cast (bind) off.
With RS facing, rejoin yarn to remaining 73 sts and work as follows:
**Next row:** Cast (bind) off 55 sts, k to end. Place a marker at each end of these 55 sts.

**Next row:** Cast (bind) off 2 sts, p12, turn and work on these 12 sts only as follows:
**Next row:** Purl.
**Next row:** K2tog, k to last 2 sts, k2tog. (10 sts)
**Next row:** Purl.
Cast (bind) off.

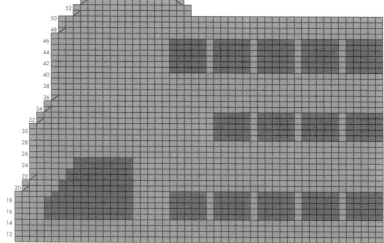

LEFT AND RIGHT SIDES

KEY

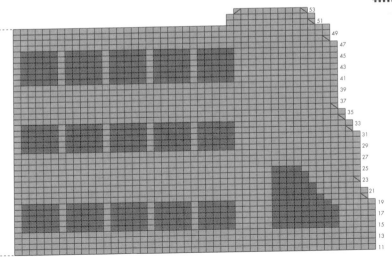

Yarn A

Yarn B

◩ ◪ Dec 1

The chart has been divided where the pages of the book join (indicated by dashed lines). Work across both sections as if they were a single chart.

**HOW TO WORK THIS CHART**

Note that both sides of the ferry are worked from the same chart, but to reverse the detail, one side is worked as normal (right side rows from right to left/wrong side rows from left to right) and the other side is worked in the opposite direction (right side rows from left to right and wrong side rows from right to left).

53
51
49
47
45
43
41
39
37
35
33
31
29
27
25
23
21
19
17
15
13
11

## FRONT

Using 4mm (US 6) needles
and A, cast on 41 sts.
**Row 1 (RS):** Knit.
**Row 2:** Purl.
Repeat last two rows sixteen
more times.
Work rows 1–32 from the front
chart provided, beginning with a
knit row and working in stocking
(stockinette) stitch (knit on RS,
purl on WS). Change colours
using the intarsia technique
as indicated.
Cast (bind) off.

## BACK

Using 4mm (US 6) needles
and A, cast on 41 sts.
**Row 1 (RS):** Knit.
**Row 2:** Purl.
Repeat last two rows fourteen
more times.
Work rows 1–32 from the back
chart provided, beginning with a
knit row and working in stocking
(stockinette) stitch (knit on RS,
purl on WS). Change colours
using the intarsia technique
as indicated.
Cast (bind) off.

**FRONT AND BACK**

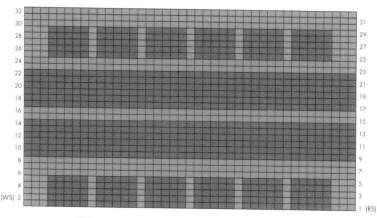

KEY  Yarn A     Yarn B

## BASE

Using 4mm (US 6) needles
and B, cast on 41 sts.
**Row 1 (RS):** Knit.
**Row 2:** Purl.
Repeat last two rows five
more times.
**Row 13:** Knit.
**Row 14:** Knit (this creates
a ridge).
**Row 15:** Knit.
**Row 16:** Purl.
Repeat last two rows until
work measures 56cm (22in)
from ridge, ending with a
WS row.
**Next row (RS):** Knit.
**Next row:** Knit (this creates
a ridge).
**Next row:** Knit.
**Next row:** Purl.
Repeat last two rows five
more times.
Cast (bind) off.

## TOP DECK

Using 4mm (US 6) needles
and B, cast on 41 sts.
**Row 1 (RS):** Knit.
**Row 2:** Purl.
Repeat last two rows until work
measures 29cm (11½in) from
cast-on edge.
Cast (bind) off.

## LARGE CABIN

Using 4mm (US 6) needles
and D, cast on 46 sts.
**Row 1 (RS):** K7, slip 1, k8,
slip 1, k12, slip 1, k8,
slip 1, k7.
**Row 2:** Purl.
Repeat last two rows twice more.
Change to C and repeat rows
1 and 2 twice more.
Cast (bind) off.

## LARGE CABIN ROOF

Using 4mm (US 6) needles
and D, cast on 41 sts.
**Row 1 (RS):** Knit.
**Row 2:** Purl.
**Row 3:** Purl (this creates a ridge).
**Row 4:** Purl.
**Row 5:** Knit.
Repeat last two rows eight
more times.
**Row 22:** Purl.
**Row 23:** Purl (this creates
a ridge).
**Row 24:** Purl.
**Row 25:** Knit.
Cast (bind) off.

## SMALL CABIN

Using 4mm (US 6) needles
and D, cast on 38 sts.
**Row 1 (RS):** K6, slip 1, k6,
slip 1, k10, slip 1, k6,
slip 1, k6.
**Row 2:** Purl.
Repeat last two rows twice more.
Change to C and repeat rows
1 and 2 twice more.
Cast (bind) off.

## SMALL CABIN ROOF

Using 4mm (US 6) needles
and D, cast on 15 sts.
**Row 1 (RS):** Knit.
**Row 2:** Purl.
**Row 3:** Purl (this creates a ridge).
**Row 4:** Purl.
**Row 5:** Knit.
Repeat last two rows seven
more times.
**Row 20:** Purl.
**Row 21:** Purl (this creates
a ridge).
**Row 22:** Purl.
**Row 23:** Knit.
Cast (bind) off.

## FUNNEL

Using 4mm (US 6) needles
and C, cast on 20 sts.
**Row 1 (RS):** Knit.
**Row 2:** Purl.
**Next row:** K10, wrap st, turn
and purl to end.
**Next row:** **Knit (getting rid
of wrapped stitch as you work
over it).
**Next row:** Purl.
**Next row:** Knit.
**Next row:** Purl.
**Next row:** Knit.
**Next row:** Purl.
**Next row:** K10, wrap st, turn
and purl to end.
Repeat from ** nine times.
**Next row:** Knit (getting rid
of wrapped stitch as you work
over it).
**Next row:** Purl.
**Next row:** Knit.
**Next row:** Purl.
Cast (bind) off.

## FUNNEL TOP

Using 4mm (US 6) needles
and C, cast on 5 sts.
**Row 1 (WS):** Purl.
**Row 2:** K1, m1, k to last st, m1,
k1. (7 sts)
Repeat last two rows until there
are 15 sts.

**Next row (WS):** Purl.
**Next row:** Knit.
**Next row:** Purl.
Repeat last two rows four
more times.
**Next row:** K2tog, k to last 2 sts,
k2tog. (13 sts)
**Next row:** Purl.
**Next row:** K2tog, k to last 2 sts,
k2tog. (11 sts)
Repeat last two rows until there
are 5 sts.
**Next row (WS):** Purl.
Cast (bind) off.

## FLAG FRONT

Using 3mm (US 2/3) needles
and F, cast on 13 sts. Change
to E and work all twelve rows
of the flag front chart provided,
beginning with a knit row and
working in stocking (stockinette)
stitch (knit on RS, purl on WS).
Change colours using the intarsia
technique as indicated. When
completed, cast (bind) off.
Embroider a few white spots
onto the blue section to create
the stars.

## FLAG BACK

Using 3mm (US 2/3) needles
and F, cast on 13 sts.
**Row 1 (RS):** Knit.
**Row 2:** Purl.
Repeat last two rows five
more times.
Cast (bind) off.

## FLAG POLE

The flag pole is made from an
i-cord. Using 2.5mm (US 1/2)
double-pointed needles and E,
cast on 3 sts. Knit every row
using the i-cord technique until
the cord measures 12cm (4¾in).
K3tog and fasten off, leaving
a long tail to sew the pole to
the flag.

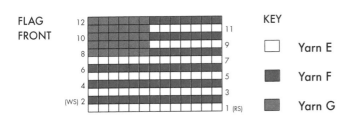

**FLAG FRONT**

12 — 11
10 — 9
8 — 7
6 — 5
4 — 3
(WS) 2 — 1 (RS)

**KEY**

☐ Yarn E

▨ Yarn F

▨ Yarn G

## FINISHING
### Main Ferry Structure

Using yarn B, embroider 'Staten Island Ferry' along both side panels of the ferry, just above the lowest row of windows.

Each end of the ferry base has a 'hem' that can be turned over along the garter stitch ridge. Fold over at the ridge and slip stitch into place on the wrong (purl) side of the work. With the right (knit) side of the base facing down so that it will be on the outside of the ferry (the purl side will be inside), sew the base to the cast-on edges of the two side panels. The sides should be positioned between the two hems, with the hems left free to create a 'platform' at each end of the ferry.

The ferry runs between Manhattan and Staten Island. The service operates 24 hours a day, every day of the year, and each crossing takes about 25 minutes.

Each side panel has a black 'cutout' at each end (in line with the lowest row of windows) and one of these cutouts is bigger than the other. The bigger one should be at the front of the ferry.

Sew the side edges of the top deck to the cast-off (bound-off) edges of the two side panels, starting and finishing at the markers. The cast-on and cast-off (bound-off) edges of the top deck should remain unattached at this point. Sew the cast-on edge of the front panel to the free edge of the top deck at the front of the ferry, then sew the side edges of the front panel to the sides of the ferry. Sew the cast-off (bound-off) edge of the front panel to the base of the ferry, along the slip stitches of the hem.

Attach the back panel to the top deck and sides of the ferry in the same way. Insert a block of foam that reaches to the top of the uppermost row of windows, then insert two smaller blocks of foam to create the increased height at each end of the top deck. Sew the final seam at the base of the back panel.

## Large and Small Cabins

The sides of the cabins are knitted all in one piece, with slipped stitches creating the four corners. Join the two side edges together to complete each structure.

Each roof has a 'hem' at each end that can be turned over along the garter stitch ridge. Fold over at the ridge and slip stitch into place on the wrong (purl) side of the work. With right (knit) side uppermost, sew the roof into place so that there is a slight overhang all the way around. Insert foam and then sew each cabin to the top of the ferry, the larger one at centre front and the smaller one at centre back.

## Funnel

The funnel is knitted sideways, with the base wider and the top narrower. Sew the funnel top to the narrower end of the funnel. Insert foam and then sew into place at the centre of the top deck.

## Flag

Sew the back and front of the flag together, hiding any untidy ends, and then attach the flag to the pole. Insert a thin piece of dowelling into the i-cord pole to encourage it to stand upright, then press the pole into the foam on the top deck near the funnel. Secure with a few stitches.

# BROADWAY STREET SIGN

## MEASUREMENTS
Height: 17cm (6¾in)
Width: 45cm (17¾in)

## YARN
Two 50g (85m/93yd) balls
of Rowan Handknit Cotton in
each of Sea Foam 352 (A) and
Bleached White 263 (B)

## MATERIALS
One pair of 4mm (US 6)
knitting needles;
Tapestry needle;
Wadding (batting)

## TENSION (GAUGE)
20 sts and 28 rows to
10cm (4in) over stocking
(stockinette) stitch using
4mm (US 6) needles.

## ABBREVIATIONS
See pages 92-95 for
abbreviations and
information on charts
and the intarsia technique.

### FRONT PANEL
Using B, cast on 89 sts.
Work all 42 rows of the front
panel chart provided, beginning
with a knit row and working
in stocking (stockinette) stitch
(knit on RS, purl on WS).
Change colours using the intarsia
technique as indicated. When
completed, cast (bind) off.

SEE PAGES 64-65
FOR FRONT
PANEL CHART

**COLOUR KEY**
Yarn A = blue green
Yarn B = white

## FRONT PANEL

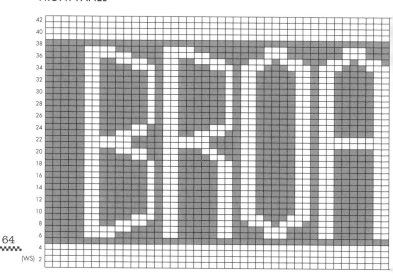

The chart has been divided where the pages of the book join (indicated by dashed lines). Work across both sections as if they were a single chart.

### BACK PANEL
Using A, cast on 89 sts.
**Row 1 (RS):** Knit.
**Row 2:** Purl.
Repeat last two rows twenty more times.
Cast (bind) off.

### FINISHING
Sew the front and back panels together using mattress stitch, working up one side, along the top, down the other side and three-quarters of the way along the bottom. Insert wadding (batting) and then finish the seam.

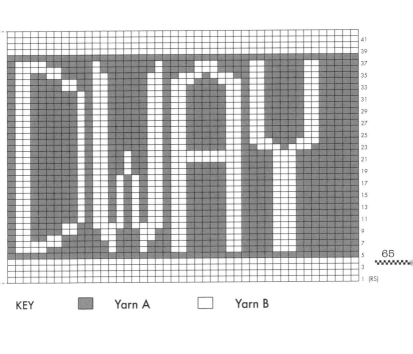

KEY    ▨ Yarn A    ☐ Yarn B

# HOT DOG

## MEASUREMENTS
Hot dog: 14.5cm (6in) long;
11cm (4in) circumference
Bread roll: 14.5cm (6in) long;
13cm (5in) at widest point
Napkin: 19 x 17cm (7½ x 6¾in)

## YARN
One 50g (130m/142yd) ball
of Rowan Pima Cotton DK
in each of Dijon 071 (A)
and Clay 075 (B);
One 50g (85m/93yd) ball
of Rowan Handknit Cotton
in Bleached 263 (C);
Small amount of Rowan Siena
4 Ply in Madras 675 (D)

## MATERIALS
One pair each of 3.25mm
(US 3) and 4mm (US 6)
knitting needles;
Two 3.25mm (US 3)
double-pointed needles
Tapestry needle;
Wadding (batting)

## TENSION (GAUGE)
24 sts and 34 rows to
10cm (4in) over stocking
(stockinette) stitch using
Rowan Pima Cotton and
3.25mm (US 3) needles.

## ABBREVIATIONS
See pages 92–95 for
abbreviations and information
on the i-cord technique.

Nathan's Famous fast
food chain, established
in 1916 on New York's
Coney Island, specializes
in hot dogs. An annual
hot dog eating contest
takes place there on
4th July. To date, the
world record is 68 hot
dogs in 10 minutes!

**COLOUR KEY**
Yarn A = beige
Yarn B = brown
Yarn C = white
Yarn D = yellow

## BREAD ROLL
### Outer Section (make 2)
Using 3.25 (US 3) needles
and A, cast on 5 sts.
**Row 1 (WS):** Purl.
**Row 2:** K1, [m1, k1] to end.
(9 sts)
Repeat last two rows once more.
(17 sts)
**Row 5:** Purl.
**Row 6:** K1, m1, k to last st, m1,
k1. (19 sts)
**Row 7:** Purl.
**Row 8:** Knit.
**Row 9:** Purl.
**Row 10:** K1, m1, k to last st,
m1, k1. (21 sts)

Repeat last two rows once more.
(23 sts)
**Row 13:** Purl.
**Row 14:** Knit.
**Row 15:** Purl.
**Row 16:** K1, m1, k to last st,
m1, k1. (25 sts)
**Row 17:** Purl.
**Row 18:** Knit.
**Row 19:** Purl.
Repeat last two rows thirteen
more times.
**Row 46:** K2tog, k to last 2 sts,
k2tog. (23 sts)
**Row 47:** Purl.
**Row 48:** Knit.
**Row 49:** Purl.

**Row 50:** K2tog, k to last 2 sts,
k2tog. (21 sts)
Repeat last four rows once more.
(19 sts)
**Row 55:** Purl.
**Row 56:** K2tog, k to last 2 sts,
k2tog. (17 sts)
**Row 57:** Purl.
**Row 58:** K1, [k2tog] to end.
(9 sts)
Repeat last two rows once more.
(5 sts)
**Row 61:** Purl.
Cast (bind) off.

**Inner Section (make 2)**
Using 3.25mm (US 3) needles
and A, cast on 5 sts.
**Row 1 (RS):** Purl.
**Row 2:** K1, [m1, k1] to end.
(9 sts)
Repeat last two rows once more.
(17 sts)
**Row 5:** Purl.
**Row 6:** K1, m1, k to last st, m1,
k1. (19 sts)
**Row 7:** Purl.
**Row 8:** Knit.

**Row 9:** Purl.
Repeat last two rows twenty-two
more times.
**Row 54:** K2tog, k to last 2 sts,
k2tog. (17 sts)
**Row 55:** Purl.
**Row 56:** K1, [k2tog] to end.
(9 sts)
Repeat last two rows once more.
(5 sts)
**Row 59:** Purl.
Cast (bind) off.

## HOT DOG

Using 3.25mm (US 3) needles and B, cast on 5 sts.

**Row 1 (WS):** Purl.
**Row 2:** K1, [m1, k1] to end. (9 sts)
Repeat last two once more. (17 sts)
**Row 5:** Purl.
**Row 6:** K1, [m1, k3] to last st, m1, k1. (23 sts)
**Row 7:** Purl.
**Row 8:** Knit.
**Row 9:** Purl.
Repeat last two rows nineteen more times.
**Row 48:** K1, [k2tog, k2] five times, k2tog. (17 sts)
**Row 49:** Purl.
**Row 50:** K1, [k2tog] to end. (9 sts)
**Row 51:** Purl.
**Row 52:** K1, [k2tog] to end. (5 sts)
Repeat last two rows once more. (3 sts)
**Row 55:** Purl.
Do not cast (bind) off. Thread yarn through remaining stitches and pull together.

## MUSTARD

The mustard is made from an i-cord. Using 3.25mm (US 3) double-pointed needles and D, cast on 3 sts. Knit every row using the i-cord technique until the cord measures 24cm (9½in). K3tog and fasten off, leaving a long tail of yarn to sew the mustard to the hot dog.

## NAPKIN

Using 4mm (US 6) needles and C, cast on 39 sts.
**Row 1 (RS):** K1, [p1, k1] to end.
This row forms moss (seed) stitch.
Repeat this row seven more times.
**Row 9:** K1, [p1, k1] twice, k to end.
**Row 10:** P to last 7 sts, k1, [p1, k1] to end.
Repeat last two rows until work measures 18cm (7in) from cast-on edge.
Cast (bind) off.

## FINISHING
### Bread Roll

The reverse stocking (stockinette) stitch side is the right side of the inner section of the bread roll; the stocking (stockinette) stitch side is the right side of the outer section of the bread roll. With wrong sides together, line up the cast-on edge of the outer section with the cast-on edge of the inner section and sew the two pieces together, leaving a small gap for stuffing. Insert wadding (batting), then finish the seam. Do this for both halves of the bread roll and then join both pieces by sewing them together along one side. You will now have an 'open' roll.

### Hot Dog

With wrong sides together, fold the hot dog in half lengthways and join the two side edges using mattress stitch, inserting wadding (batting) as you go along. This will form a long sausage shape.

Sew the mustard to the top of the hot dog in a zigzag pattern. Place the hot dog into the bread roll and stitch into place, then place the roll onto the napkin.

# FIRE HYDRANT

## MEASUREMENTS
Height: 26cm (10¼in)
Circumference: 27cm (10¾in)

## YARN
Three 50g (115m/126yd)
balls of Rowan Cotton Glace
in Poppy 741

## MATERIALS
One pair of 3mm
(US 2/3) knitting needles;
Two 3.25mm (US 3) and
two 3.75mm (US 5)
double-pointed needles;
Five stitch markers;
Tapestry needle;
Plastic tube, such as a
water bottle, approx. 27cm
(10¾in) circumference;
Wadding (batting)

## TENSION (GAUGE)
26 sts and 34 rows to 10cm
(4in) measured over stocking
(stockinette) stitch using
3mm (US 2/3) needles.

## ABBREVIATIONS
See pages 92–95 for
abbreviations and information
on the i-cord technique.

In the late 19th century,
firemen in New York City
were known colloquially
as Johnnies, and fire
hydrants became known
as johnny pumps.

## MAIN CYLINDER

Using 3mm (US 2/3) needles, cast on 80 sts.

**Row 1 (RS):** K3, [p3, k3] to last 5 sts, p3, k2.

**Row 2:** P2, [k3, p3] to end.

Repeat last two rows until work measures 19cm (7½in) from cast-on edge, ending with a WS row.

Cast (bind) off in pattern.

## BASE

Using 3mm (US 2/3) needles, cast on 9 sts.

**Row 1 (WS):** Purl.

**Row 2:** K1, m1, k to last st, m1, k1. (11 sts)

Repeat last two rows until you have 23 sts.

**Next row:** Purl.

**Next row:** Knit.

**Next row:** Purl.

**Next row:** Knit.

**Next row:** Purl.

**Next row:** K2tog, k to last 2 sts, k2tog. (21 sts)

Repeat last two rows until you have 9 sts.

**Next row:** Purl.

Cast (bind) off.

## BASE RING

Using 3mm (US 2/3) needles, cast on 13 sts.

**Row 1 (RS):** K4, p1, k3, p1, k4.

**Row 2:** P4, k1, p3, k1, p4.

Repeat last two rows until work measures 34cm (13½in) from cast-on edge, ending with a WS row.

Cast (bind) off in pattern.

## TOP – 'HAT' SECTION

Using 3mm (US 2/3) needles, cast on 80 sts.

**Row 1 (RS):** K3, [p3, k3] to last 5 sts, p3, k2.

**Row 2:** P2, [k3, p3] to end.

Repeat last two rows three more times.

**Row 9:** [K3, p1, p2tog] to last 2 sts, k2. (67 sts)

**Row 10:** P2, [k2, p3] to end.

**Row 11:** K3, [p2, k3] to last 4 sts, p2, k2.

**Row 12:** P2, [k2, p3] to end.

**Row 13:** K1, k2tog, [p2, k1, k2tog] to last 4 sts, p2, k2tog. (53 sts)

**Row 14:** P1, [k2, p2] to end.

**Row 15:** [K2, p2] to last st, k1.

**Row 16:** P1, [k2, p2] to end.

**Row 17:** K2, [p2tog, k2] to last 3 sts, p2tog, k1. (40 sts)

**Row 18:** P1, [k1, p2] to end.

**Row 19:** [K2, p1] to last st, k1.

**Row 20:** P1, [k1, p2] to end.
**Row 21:** [K2tog, p1] to last st, k1. (27 sts)
**Row 22:** P1, [k1, p1] to end.
**Row 23:** K1, [p1, k1] to end.
**Row 24:** P1, [k1, p1] to end.
Do not cast (bind) off. Thread yarn through remaining stitches and pull together.

## TOP – 'BRIM' SECTION
The brim is made from three i-cords.

### Small i-cord
Using 3.25mm (US 3) double-pointed needles, cast on 5 sts. Knit every row using the i-cord technique until the cord measures 29cm (11½in). Cast (bind) off, knitting two stitches together at each end.

### Medium i-cord
Using 3.75mm (US 5) double-pointed needles and yarn held double, cast on 5 sts. Knit every row using the i-cord technique until the cord measures 33cm (13in). Cast (bind) off, knitting two stitches together at each end.

### Large i-cord
Using 3.75mm (US 5) double-pointed needles and yarn held double, cast on 5 sts. Knit every row using the i-cord technique until the cord measures 36cm (14in). Cast (bind) off, knitting two stitches together at each end.

## VALVE – SMALL (make 2)
Using 3mm (US 2/3) needles, cast on 31 sts.
**Row 1 (RS):** Knit.
**Row 2:** Purl.
Repeat last two rows once more. Place markers on the 9th, 16th and 23rd stitches.
**Row 5:** K1, k2tog, k to last 3 sts decreasing one stitch at either side of each marked stitch, k2tog, k1. (23 sts)
**Row 6:** Purl.
**Row 7:** Knit.
**Row 8:** Purl.
**Row 9:** K1, k2tog, k to last 3 sts decreasing one stitch at either side of each marked stitch, k2tog, k1. (15 sts)
**Row 10:** Purl.
**Row 11:** [Slip 2, k1, p2sso] to end. (5 sts)
Do not cast (bind) off. Thread yarn through remaining stitches and pull together.

## VALVE – LARGE

Using 3mm (US 2/3) needles, cast on 45 sts.

**Row 1 (RS):** Knit.

**Row 2:** Purl.

Repeat last two rows once more. Place markers on the 9th, 16th, 23rd, 30th and 37th stitches.

**Row 5:** K1, k2tog, k to last 3 sts decreasing one stitch at either side of each marked stitch, k2tog, k1. (33 sts)

**Row 6:** Purl.

**Row 7:** Knit.

**Row 8:** Purl.

**Row 9:** K1, k2tog, k to last 3 sts decreasing one stitch at either side of each marked stitch, k2tog, k1. (21 sts)

**Row 10:** Purl.

**Row 11:** [Slip 2, k1, p2sso] to end. (7 sts)

Do not cast (bind) off. Thread yarn through remaining stitches and pull together.

## FINISHING
### Main Cylinder

Join the two side edges of the main cylinder using mattress stitch. Insert the plastic tube to enable the hydrant to stand up. Sew the base to the cast-on edge of the main cylinder. Fold the base ring in half lengthways and join the two side edges using mattress stitch; this will form a tube. Insert wadding (batting) and join the two ends of the tube by sewing the cast-on edge to the cast-off (bound-off) edge to form a ring. Place the main cylinder of the hydrant inside the ring. The ring should be a snug fit so that it stays in place. If loose, sew it into place.

### Top Section

Join the side edges of the top 'hat' section using mattress stitch. You now need to sew the three i-cords around the base of the 'hat' section to create the 'brim'. For each i-cord, join the cast-on edge to the cast-off (bound-off) edge to form three separate rings. Sew the smallest i-cord ring to the cast-on edge of the top 'hat' section. Sew the medium i-cord ring around the bottom of the small i-cord ring, then sew the large i-cord ring around the bottom of the medium i-cord ring. Stuff the assembled top section with wadding (batting), then position the top section onto the main cylinder and slip stitch it into place.

## Valves

Insert a little bit of wadding (batting) into each of the valves, then sew the valves into place. The two small valves should be on opposite sides of the hydrant, about a quarter of the way down the main cylinder. The large valve should be at the centre front, about a third of the way down the main cylinder.

A PLASTIC WATER BOTTLE IS IDEAL AS THE INNER TUBE SUPPORT

# FLATIRON BUILDING

## MEASUREMENTS

Height: 50cm (19½in)
Width: 15cm (6in) across back
Length: 23cm (9in) along side

## YARN

Three 50g (85m/93yd) balls
of Rowan Handknit Cotton in
Linen 205 (A) and two
balls in Slate 347 (B)

## MATERIALS

One pair of 4mm (US 6)
knitting needles;
Foam and wadding (batting)

## TENSION (GAUGE)

20 sts and 28 rows to 10cm
(4in) measured over stocking
(stockinette) stitch using
4mm (US 6) needles.

## ABBREVIATIONS

See pages 92–95 for
abbreviations and information
on charts and the Fair Isle
(stranding) technique.

## NOTE

Slip all slipped stitches purlwise.

Completed in 1902, the
wedge-shaped Flatiron
Building is named for its
resemblance to an old-
fashioned clothes iron.

**COLOUR KEY**
Yarn A = beige
Yarn B = grey

## SIDES

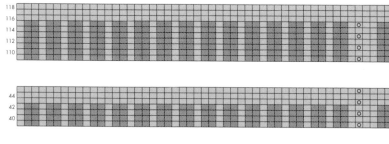

(WS)

**SIDES (knitted in one piece)**
Using A, cast on 100 sts.
**Row 1 (RS):** K46, slip 1, k6,
slip 1, k46.
**Row 2:** Purl.
Work rows 3–10 from the sides
chart provided, beginning with a
knit row and working in stocking
(stockinette) stitch (knit on RS,
purl on WS) unless indicated
otherwise. Change colours using
the Fair Isle (stranding) technique
as indicated.
**Row 11:** Knit.
**Row 12:** Purl.
**Row 13:** P46, yb, slip 1, yfwd,
p6, yb, slip 1, yfwd, p46.
**Row 14:** Purl.

Repeat rows 3–14 twice more.
Work rows 39–45 from the chart
nine times and then rows 39–43
once again.
**Row 107 (RS):** Purl.
**Row 108:** Purl.
Work rows 109–118 from
the chart.
Cast (bind) off.

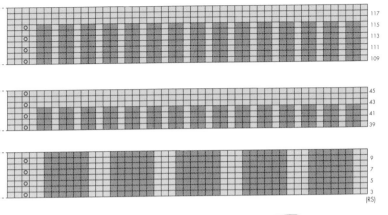

KEY

☐ Yarn A

■ Yarn B

◯ Slip 1 purlwise

The chart has been divided where the pages of the book join (indicated by dashed lines). Work across both sections as if they were a single chart.

# BACK

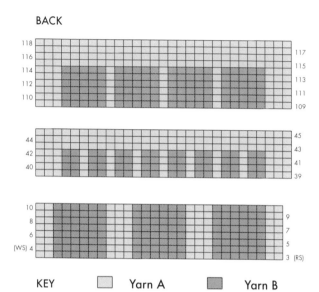

**KEY** ☐ Yarn A   ☐ Yarn B

**BACK**
Using A, cast on 28 sts.
**Row 1 (RS):** Knit.
**Row 2:** Purl.
Work rows 3–10 from the back chart provided, beginning with a knit row and working in stocking (stockinette) stitch (knit on RS, purl on WS). Change colours using the Fair Isle (stranding) technique as indicated.
**Row 11:** Knit.
**Row 12:** Purl.
**Row 13:** Purl.
**Row 14:** Purl.
Repeat rows 3–14 once more and then rows 3–13 once again.
**Row 38:** Purl, increasing one stitch in the centre of the row. (29 sts)
Work rows 39–45 from the chart nine times and then rows 39–43 once again.
**Row 107 (RS):** Purl.
**Row 108:** Purl.
Work rows 109–118 from the chart.
Cast (bind) off.

## BASE

Using A, cast on 29 sts.
**Row 1 (RS):** Knit.
**Row 2:** Purl.
**Row 3:** Knit.
**Row 4:** Purl.
**Row 5:** K2tog, k to last 2 sts, k2tog. (27 sts)
**Row 6:** Purl.
**Row 7:** Knit.
**Row 8:** Purl.
**Row 9:** K2tog, k to last 2 sts, k2tog. (25 sts)
Repeat last two rows until 1 st remains and fasten off.

## ROOF

Work as for base.

## FINISHING

Sew the side edges of the back to the side edges of the sides. Insert the foam and then sew the base into place. The shape of the front corner of the building has been created using slipped stitches. If you want to accentuate this shape, insert some wadding (batting) into this corner. Sew the roof into place.

# WALK/DON'T WALK

## MEASUREMENTS
Height: 45cm (17¾in)
Width: 45cm (17¾in)
Depth: 10cm (4in)

## YARN
Six 50g (85m/93yd) balls of
Rowan Handknit Cotton in
Black 252 (A) and three balls
in each of Slate 347 (B) and
Bleached 263 (C);
One 100g (274m/300yd)
ball of Patons Fab DK
in Canary 2305 (D)

## MATERIALS
One pair of 4mm (US 6)
knitting needles;
Tapestry needle;
Foam

## TENSION (GAUGE)
20 sts and 28 rows to
10cm (4in) over stocking
(stockinette) stitch using
Rowan Handknit Cotton and
4mm (US 6) needles.

## ABBREVIATIONS
See pages 92-95 for
abbreviations and
information on charts
and the intarsia technique.

**COLOUR KEY**
Yarn A = black
Yarn B = grey
Yarn C = white
Yarn D = yellow

## FRONT PANEL

Using A, cast on 89 sts.
Work all 122 rows of the
front chart provided, beginning
with a knit row and working
in stocking (stockinette) stitch
(knit on RS, purl on WS).
Change colours using the intarsia
technique as indicated. When
completed, cast (bind) off.

## BACK PANEL

Using A, cast on 89 sts.
Work all 122 rows of the
back chart provided, beginning
with a knit row and working
in stocking (stockinette) stitch
(knit on RS, purl on WS).
Change colours using the intarsia
technique as indicated. When
completed, cast (bind) off.

## SIDE GUSSET

Using D, cast on 23 sts.
**Row 1 (RS):** Knit.
**Row 2:** Purl.
Repeat last two rows until work
measures 180cm (71in) from
cast-on edge. Check to make
sure that it will fit around all four
sides of the front/back pieces,
then cast (bind) off.

## FINISHING

Sew the side edges of the gusset
to the edges of the front panel.
Start in the middle of the cast-on
row of the front and work all the
way around until you get back to
where you started. Then attach
the back panel to the other side
edge in the same way, leaving
a large gap for stuffing. Insert
foam, then finish the seam.

SEE PAGES 88-91
FOR CHARTS

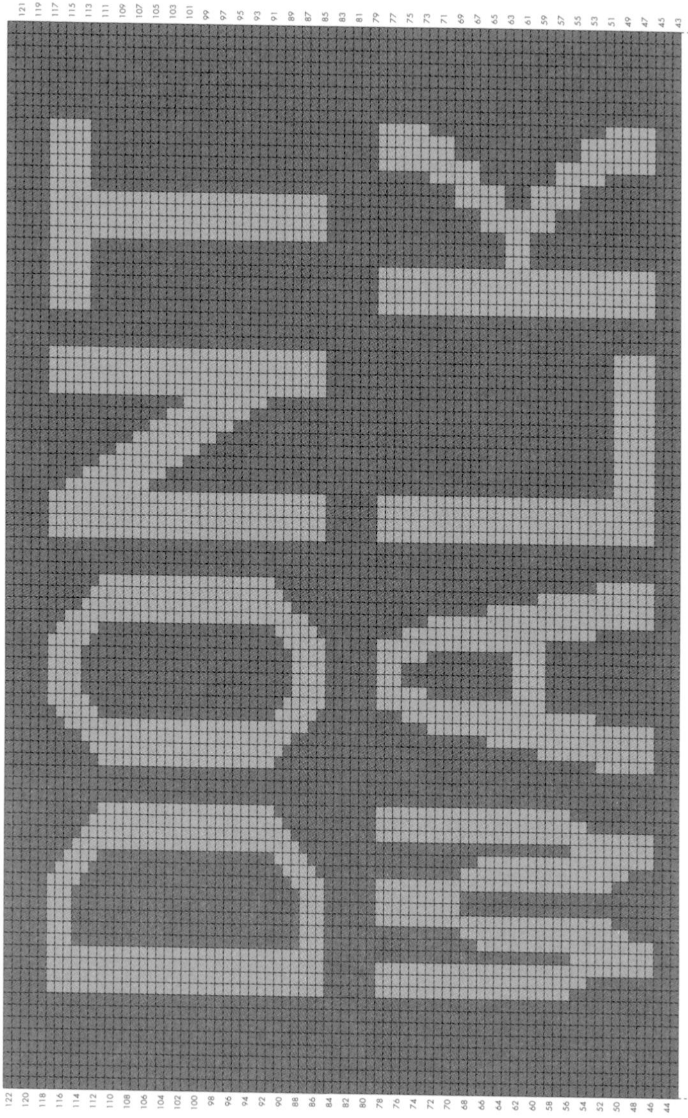

KEY

■ Yarn A

■ Yarn B

□ Yarn C

The chart has been divided where the pages of the book join (indicated by dashed lines). Work across both sections as if they were a single chart.

89

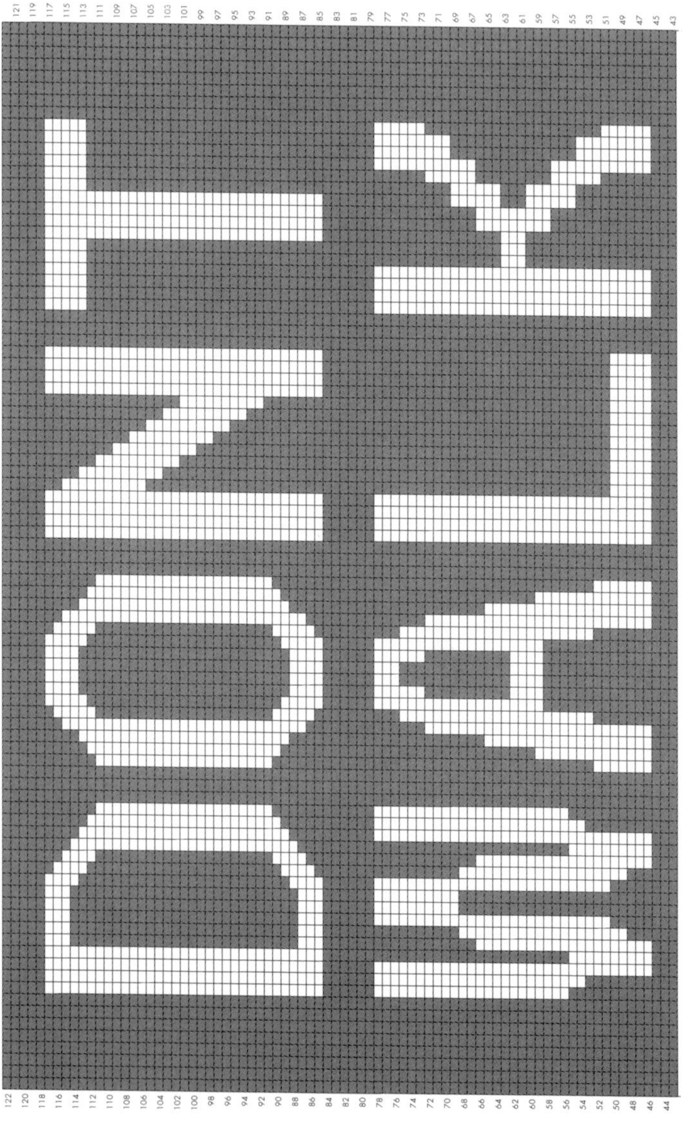
121 119 117 115 113 111 109 107 105 103 101 99 97 95 93 91 89 87 85 83 81 79 77 75 73 71 69 67 65 63 61 59 57 55 53 51 49 47 45 43
122 120 118 116 114 112 110 108 106 104 102 100 98 96 94 92 90 88 86 84 82 80 78 76 74 72 70 68 66 64 62 60 58 56 54 52 50 48 46 44

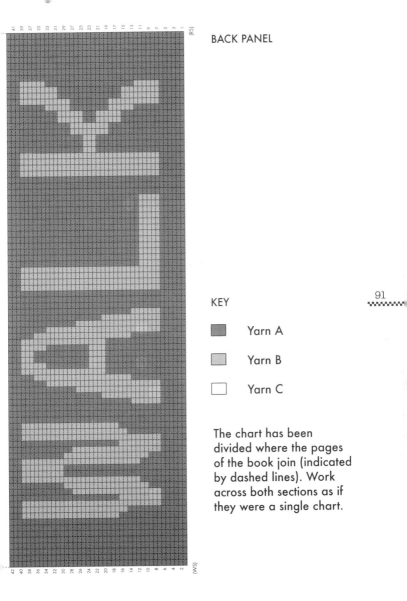

BACK PANEL

KEY

■ Yarn A

□ Yarn B

□ Yarn C

The chart has been divided where the pages of the book join (indicated by dashed lines). Work across both sections as if they were a single chart.

# TECHNIQUES

All of the abbreviations and special techniques
used in the patterns are explained here.

## ABBREVIATIONS

**approx:** approximately

**cm:** centimetre(s)

**dec 1:** decrease one stitch by working k2tog or p2tog

**g:** gram(s)

**in:** inch(es)

**inc 1:** increase one stitch by knitting or purling into front and then back of same stitch

**k:** knit

**k2(3)tog:** knit two (three) stitches together

**m1:** make one stitch: put the tip of the left needle from front to back under the horizontal strand of yarn that stretches between the stitch just worked and the next stitch; pick up this strand with the left needle and knit or purl through the back of it to create an extra stitch on the right needle, then slip the strand off the left needle

**mm:** millimetre(s)

**p:** purl

**p2sso:** pass two slipped stitches over stitch(es) just worked and off needle

**p2tog:** purl two stitches together

**rep:** repeat

**RS:** right side

**slip 1(2):** slip specified number of stitches from the left to the right needle without working them; all stitches in the projects are slipped purlwise

**st(s):** stitch(es)

**tog:** together

**WS:** wrong side

**yb:** take yarn between needles to back of work

**yfwd:** bring yarn between needles to front of work

**\*** work instructions after asterisk(s) as directed

**[ ]** work instructions within square brackets as directed

## WORKING FROM CHARTS

All of the charts in this book are worked in stocking (stockinette) stitch (knit on RS rows, purl on WS rows) unless indicated otherwise. A key is provided to explain different stitch instructions and show which yarn colours to use. Unless indicated otherwise, work each chart from the bottom upwards, reading all RS rows from right to left and all WS rows from left to right.

## COLOUR KNITTING

There are two main techniques for working with more than one colour in the same row of knitting: the intarsia technique and the Fair Isle (stranding) technique.

### Intarsia Technique

Use the intarsia technique when knitting individual, large blocks of colour. It is best to use a small ball or long length of yarn for each area of colour, otherwise the yarns will easily become tangled. When changing to a new colour, twist the yarns on the WS to prevent a hole from forming.

When starting a new row, turn the knitting so that the yarns that are hanging from it untwist as much as possible. If you have several colours, you may occasionally have to reorganize the yarns at the back of the knitting. Your work may look messy, but once the ends are all sewn in it will look fine.

### Fair Isle (Stranding) Technique

If there are no more than four stitches between colours, you can use the Fair Isle (stranding) technique. Begin knitting with the first colour, then drop this when you introduce the second colour. When you come to the first colour again, take it under the second colour to twist the yarns. When you come to the second colour again, take it over the first colour. The secret is not to pull the strands on the wrong side of the work too tightly, or the work will pucker.

## WRAP STITCH

Sometimes a pattern requires you to turn the work partway through a row. Working a wrap stitch avoids a hole from forming where the row is turned.

**Wrapping a stitch on a knit row:** Bring the yarn forward between the needles, slip a stitch purlwise from the left needle to the right needle, take the yarn back between the needles and then return the slipped stitch to the left needle.

**Wrapping a stitch on a purl row:** Take the yarn back between the needles, slip a stitch purlwise from the left to the right needle, bring the yarn forward between the needles and then return the slipped stitch to the left needle.

**Getting rid of a wrap stitch:** When the turning rows have been completed, use this technique to disguise the loops that appear around the wrapped stitches. Work up to the wrap stitch and insert the right needle up through the front (on a knit row) or back (on a purl row) of the wrap. At the same time, put the needle through the stitch directly above the wrap and work the two together.

## I-CORDS

Several of the patterns in this book use i-cords to make a variety of features. To make an i-cord, cast on the specified number of stitches using double-pointed needles.

**Row 1 (RS):** Knit.

You would now usually turn the needles to work the next row, but to make an i-cord DO NOT TURN. Instead, slide the stitches to the other end of the double-pointed needle, ready to be knitted again. The yarn will now be at the left edge of the knitting, and so to knit the next row you must pull the yarn tightly across the back of the work and then knit one more row. Continue in this way, never turning and always sliding the work to the other end of the double-pointed needle. The right side of the work will always be facing you. Repeat row 1 until the cord measures the required length. Break off the yarn, thread it through stitches and pull together to complete the cord (or finish off as specified in the pattern).

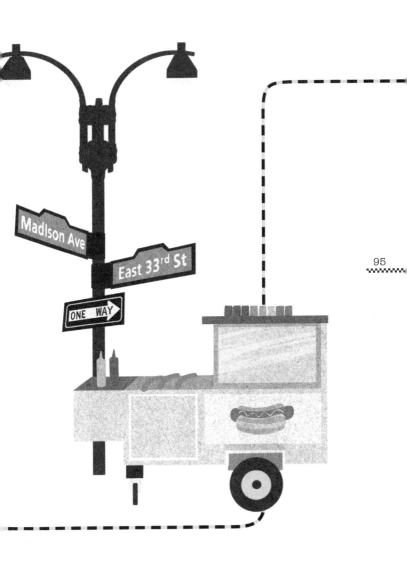

95

## YARN SUPPLIERS

www.knitrowan.com
www.patonsyarns.com
www.coatscrafts.co.uk

## AUTHOR THANKS

I would like to thank Coats Crafts for allowing me to use their wonderful yarns and to Sharon Brant and Kate Buller for their continued support. Thanks to Jez for his love, patience, calming words and once again, his attention to detail, which helped me to bring the projects to life! Thanks also to Rachel Atkinson and Michelle Pickering for their meticulous attention to detail.

## ANSWERS TO QUIZ NEW YORK (PAGE 23)

1. Queens (largest), Brooklyn, Staten Island, the Bronx and Manhattan (smallest).
2. Broadway, Seventh Avenue, 42nd Street and 47th Street.
3. Baseball: New York Yankees and New York Mets. American football: New York Giants and New York Jets.
4. Officially 468, but 421 if all transfer stations are counted as only one station (some station complexes are officially counted as two or more) – we couldn't resist a tricky one!

COLLINS & BROWN

BOOKS FOR BUSY HANDS

WWW.LOVECRAFTS.CO.UK

Join our crafting community at LoveCrafts – we look forward to meeting you!

Also available in this series: Knit London (978-1-908449-08-5). Visit our website at www.lovecrafts.co.uk for more information.